W9-CGN-710

HOW IT HAPPENS
at the Fireworks Factory

By Megan Rocker

Photographs by Bob and Diane Wolfe

CLARA HOUSE BOOKS

Minneapolis

THE NYACK LIBRARY

The publisher would like to thank Precocious Pyrotechnics, Inc., and its employees for their generous help with this book.

All photographs by Bob and Diane Wolfe except p. 31 (courtesy Precocious Pyrotechnics, Inc.).

Copyright ©2004 by Clara House Books, a division of The Oliver Press, Inc.
All rights reserved.
No part of this book may be reproduced in any form or by any means without permission in writing from the publisher. Please address inquiries to:

Clara House Books
The Oliver Press, Inc.
Charlotte Square
5707 West 36th Street
Minneapolis, MN 55416-2510

Library of Congress Cataloging-in-Publication Data
Rocker, Megan, 1976-
    How it happens at the fireworks factory / by Megan Rocker; photographs by Bob and
  Diane Wolfe.
      p. cm.
    ISBN 1-881508-97-8 (lib. bdg.)
    1. Fireworks—Juvenile literature. I. Wolfe, Robert L., ill. II. Wolfe, Diane, ill. III. Title.

TP300.R66 2004
662'.1—dc22

                                                    2004043908

ISBN 1-881508-97-8
Printed in the United States of America
10 09 08 07 06 05 04   8 7 6 5 4 3 2 1

The booms and bright colors of fireworks are a familiar part of many celebrations. But there is more to a fireworks display than the explosions you see and hear. Come along for a behind-the-scenes look at how one company makes fireworks, plans a show, and then puts on an exciting display.

Black Powder

Fireworks explode because they are made with a kind of gunpowder called **black powder**. This picture shows some of the ingredients that are used to make it. Black powder is very dangerous, so it has to be mixed carefully by trained workers.

Stars and Inserts

Imagine you are watching a fireworks display. Each firework you see is made up of multiple explosions. These are created by **igniting** (setting on fire) many small pellets made of black powder mixed with chemicals. Different chemicals can make the explosions different colors.

These pellets can be different shapes (like balls, cubes, or tubes) depending on the type of firework. Some pellets are called **stars**. To make round stars, black powder, chemicals, and water are placed in tubs that spin very quickly. This rolls the mixture into small balls.

Other pellets are called **inserts**. To make them, a mixture of black powder and chemicals is poured into paper tubes or holes on a metal rack. The rack is placed in a special machine that presses down hard on it. This forms the mixture into the shape of the holes.

Assembly

The stars and inserts are placed inside a plastic or cardboard container to make a firework, also known as a **shell**. Shells can be many different shapes and sizes. The number and arrangement of stars or inserts inside them can be different too. This is one way to create the variety you see in a fireworks display.

For example, these round stars are poured into a round container. When the finished shell explodes, the ignited stars will create a pattern like the one shown at right.

Not all inserts are loaded directly into containers. Tube-shaped inserts are often encased in thick cardboard covers first. The covers sometimes have holes drilled in them. These holes can help create sound effects (like humming or whistling) when the fireworks explode. They can also hold a **fuse**—a cord that is ignited to make the insert explode. This picture shows some covers (lower left corner) and the machine that drills the holes.

After being covered, the inserts are arranged in a container.

A filling is scooped into the empty space in the container to hold the inserts in place. The filling shown here is made of ground-up corncobs.

Next, a worker pours in rice hulls coated with black powder. This mixture is called **break powder**. When it is lit, it will help the shell explode and ignite the inserts.

After the break powder is added, a lid with a fuse is put on.

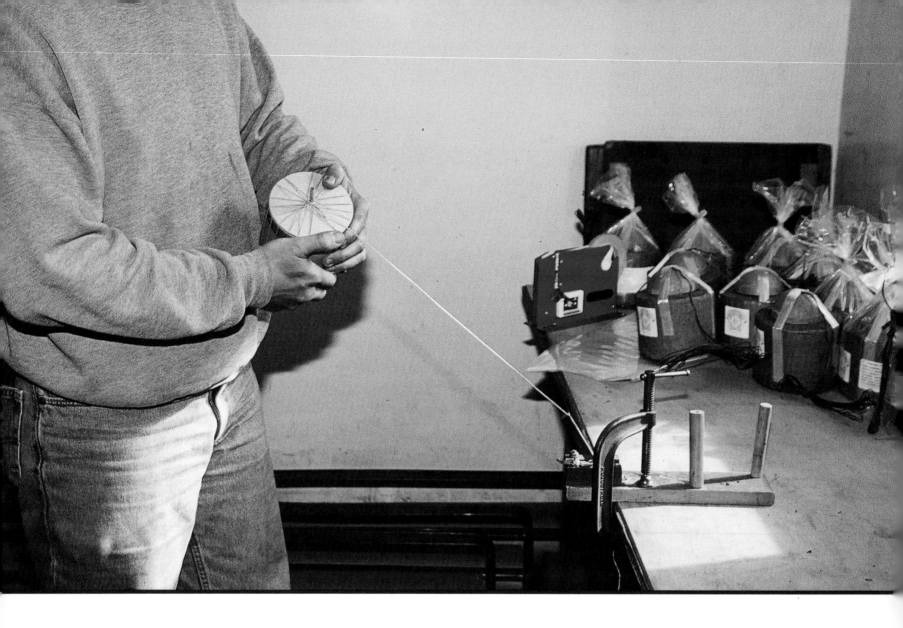

The next step is to strengthen the shell. First, it is wrapped in string (this also holds the lid on).

Then a worker spreads paste on a sheet of paper and wraps it around the shell.

The worker
finishes putting
the paper on and
sets the shell
aside to dry.

Fuses

There are many different kinds of fuses. Some are short and others are long. Some burn slowly, while others burn very quickly. These things control how long it will take a shell to explode once the fuse is lit. Sometimes more than one fuse is needed to do this. Here, a worker is adding a second fuse to the top of these shells.

This machine makes fuses by coating pieces of string with black powder. The strings are fed through tubes to keep them separate, and the powder is poured over them. Later they will be wrapped in paper.

You can see the long, paper-covered fuses on these finished fireworks.

Display

This company not only makes fireworks, but it also puts on fireworks displays. The first step in doing this is to plan what the display will look like. The planner must decide how many and what kinds of fireworks to use, when each will be fired, and sometimes how to match the explosions with music. This can be a complicated task, so it is often done on a computer.

Shooting off fireworks is a dangerous job done by a crew of specially trained workers. An average 15-minute display can take about 6 hours to set up, so the workers have to get there early. When they arrive at the display site, they use a detailed plan to arrange the equipment.

The shells are launched out of tubes called **mortars**. In this display, the mortars used for the main part of the show will be set up on a truck. Others, including those used for the **finale** (end of the show) will be arranged in racks on the ground.

Metal rods hammered into the ground hold the racks steady during the display.

Next, the shells are unpacked from boxes.

Each shell is set on top of its mortar.

Every shell has a set of special wires called an **electric match** attached to its fuse. A worker connects the electric match to the firing system. There are about 300 shells in this set of racks, which means a lot of wires! They will all be straightened out and placed under the platform before the show begins.

The electric matches are wired into firing panels called **lats**. A cable connects the lats to the equipment that runs the display.

After all the wiring is done, the shells are loaded into the mortar tubes.

Some fireworks displays are run entirely by computers. Others, like this one, need an operator to tell the firing system when to fire the shells. He may follow a written plan or receive instructions over a radio. When he presses a button on the equipment, it sends an electrical signal through a lat to one of the electric matches. This creates a spark that ignites the shell's fuse, creates an explosion, and launches the firework into the air.

As the shell is launched, another fuse on it has begun burning. This fuse will ignite the break powder and stars or inserts, making the shell explode in the air and creating the familiar colors and noise of a fireworks display.

Glossary

black powder: the explosive powder used in fireworks. It is made up of potassium nitrate, sulfur, and charcoal.

break powder: a mixture of black powder and other materials that helps explode the shell

electric match: a set of special coated wires used to ignite fireworks. An electric match connects a shell's fuse to the firing system.

finale: the end of a fireworks display, when many fireworks are exploded at the same time

fuse: a cord that is lit at one end and burns down to ignite something at the other end. Fuses on fireworks often use black powder.

igniting: setting something on fire

inserts: small pellets made of black powder and chemicals, often wrapped in cardboard, that burn to make a firework's flame and color. Some tube-shaped inserts can be made to create sound effects when they burn.

lats: panels connecting electric matches to the equipment that runs a fireworks display

mortars: tubes from which shells are launched

shell: the main body of a firework

stars: small pellets, made of black powder and chemicals, that burn to make a firework's flame and color. Stars can be many shapes, such as balls or cubes.